Of Samoan, Tuvaluan, English and French descent, Selina Tusitala
Marsh was the first Pacific Islander to graduate with a PhD in English
from the University of Auckland and is now a lecturer in the English
Department, specialising in Pasifika literature. Her first collection,
the bestselling *Fast Talking PI* (Auckland University Press), won
the NZSA Jessie Mackay Award for Best First Book of Poetry in
2010. Marsh represented Tuvalu at the London Olympics Poetry
Parnassus event in 2012. Her work has been translated into Ukrainian
and Spanish and has appeared in numerous forms in schools, museums
and parks, on billboards, and in print and online literary journals.

# DARK SPARRING

## POEMS

### SELINA TUSITALA MARSH

AUCKLAND
UNIVERSITY
PRESS

First published 2013

Auckland University Press
University of Auckland
Private Bag 92019
Auckland 1142
New Zealand
www.press.auckland.ac.nz

Text © Selina Tusitala Marsh, 2013
Audio © Selina Tusitala Marsh and Tim Page, 2013
All poems written and performed by Selina Tusitala Marsh;
all music composed, produced and engineered by Tim Page.

ISBN 978 1 86940 786 5

Publication is kindly assisted by

National Library of New Zealand Cataloguing-in-Publication Data
Marsh, Selina Tusitala.
Dark sparring : poems / Selina Tusitala Marsh.
ISBN 978-1-86940-786-5
1. Grief—Poetry. I. Title.
NZ821.3—dc 23

Cover design: Spencer Levine
Cover image: Lonnie Hutchinson, details of *Before Sunrise*, 2010, builder's paper;
photograph by Sam Hartnett

Printed in China by 1010 Printing International Ltd

# CONTENTS

*The fight is won or lost far away from witnesses –*
*behind the lines, in the gym, and out there on the road,*
*long before I dance under these lights.*
– Muhammad Ali


*E lei ma saka taua?*
– a Tuvaluan invitation to dance

# MATARIKI

Matariki walks into Otahuhu Library
pretty in uniformed white and burgundy
school bag over her shoulder
red teuila behind her ear
she sits down regally among a sea
of white-capped collared students

she asks
*Ms, what's Matariki all about?*
*what's writing poems got to do with it?*
*why's the Maori new year celebrated now and here?*
*and who cares if the Pleiades shift?*

I said
*write what you remember*
*write your lost and found*
*write the toiling of the year's grief*
*write the seeding of new ground*

Matariki turned the land of her body
and breezed
*I lost my mum in January this year*
*and I really, really miss her*

Matariki and me
like black stars shooting
we soared the heavens for lost mums
and new beginnings

we saw their spirit
in that blue star shine
it glowed across Matariki's hand
and spread towards mine

in muted milky-way HB
Matariki wrote her swirling vortex down
and I read of Rihanna, songbird warrior
and of her prince, Chris Brown

of how Chris had hit and hit
the diamond love of his life
a black eye, a fat lip
scars on the inside

Matariki penned Rihanna's defeat
not of being hit, but of going back
of how *Woman's Weekly* recorded the retreat
of Songbird Queen trumped by Jack

I asked about the poem's relevance
and Matariki said
*my mum would never let that be me*
*Chris Brown? He'd be dead*

*she'd swoop in with her six sisters*
*make each of his nineteen years pay*
*they'd black-hole the arrogance out of anyone*
*who'd treat their Matariki that way*

I watched Matariki
pretty in burgundy
come into her name that day

I knew a star in blue
enlarged by two
when it heard what her poem had to say

# PART I

## CHANT FROM MATIATIA TO ORAPIU

sea skin sheening
    low clouds keening
        Fuller's disembowelling
            white scarves towelling
                Te Atawhai reserving
                    bus lines reversing
                        cafés people grinding
                            maps finger finding
                                sandals bus stopping
                                    shops hard rocking
                lazy lattes lounging on a sea-green couch

           Red Cross band aiding
        St Paul's prayers for ailing
mother earth cascading
        drives garage saling
           Fossil Bay refuelling
                dirt track view-ruling
                    tyres round-a-bouting
                      scallop shells shouting
                        toetoe cliff topping
                            beach store bottle shopping
                              Bevan's pizza firing
                                dragon's breath for hiring
                  Little 'O' drifting out of the bay

           hikers Punga Lodging
              Esplanade hole dodging
                Piritahi Blackpooling
                    kohanga reo schooling
              Samoans fast talking
            Tongans power walking
         Sue's palaver-loving

Enclosure Bay enfolding
sandy stingray moulding
Needle Point stitching
missed bus hitching
Janet's got a bird in the hand

Miami Ave vicing
speck-o'-seaview pricing
watertanks imploding
Hugh's Takeaways offloading
Neil's manipulating
billboard debating
school-cool kids spitting
orange cones night shifting
speed cameras causewaying
hurried drivers praying on the long, straight, narrow

John's tapa talking
metaphoric stalking
nudey beach reclining
Red Shed sirening
horizon line beguiling canvassed minds

houseboats duck feeding
Ostend rugby leaguing
Waiheke Rams inspiring
Anzac Bay retiring
market stalls bejewelling
Midway Motelling
Sing Tao Takeawaying
Pukeko Road signing
Get Stuffed dining
old timer's pining
council office queuing
greenbelt guards spewing

surveyors plotting
land-lubbers allotting

supermarket squatting
parked cars rashing
transfer station trashing
Levi Hawken's grinding at the skateboard park

headless tiger flexing
fuming motors vexing
one tree mountain standing
dozer teeth man-handling
agents picket signing
cyclists white lining
bridge wetlanding
Whakanewha bandstanding
horses Rocky Baying
flounder seabed raying
ti trees flag poling
tidal pools consoling sore red feet

Kina Backpacking
llamas bush tracking
motorway golf coursing
vineyard valley morselling
graves grass laying
woolsheds fraying
barber candystriping
gravel windscreen wiping

Onetangi supining
blue sky divining
lavalava lifting
dunes shape shifting

pohutukawa latching
honeymooners baching
tui reed thatching
cigars light-matching on mudbricked walls

sheep navel gazing
hills boulder grazing
Stony Batter frying
torches fading, dying
tunnels networking
cows fly jerking
kereru berry flirting
roads loop looping
sparrows hula hooping
geckos asphalt hissing
olive groves kissing
grapes wine sunning
Clive Wharf 2 Wharf running
Orapiu poking out its piered planked tongue

# AIRPORT ROAD TO APIA

*Mulifanua*
tarmac sleeping
low clouds steaming
planes disembowelling
hot babies howling
wrapping women shushing
ballpoint ticketing
wooden pe'a bulging
Afio Mai muralling the far side wall

*Satapuala*
long grass saluting
golf course polluting
lavalavas breezing
puletasi leaving
feet bus stopping
pastors flocking
a young girl slicking a rainbow slushy

*Faleasi'u*
black pig snorting
rubbish over roasting
fat man scratching
white washing waving
tomb tooth sunning
church abacusing
holy chickens tithing in the pock-marked yard

8

*Vaiusu*
lean bikes locking
au talavou singing
iron gates divining
'fessing rocks spilling

lolly Hondas filling
fales turtle-backing
children lagooning
houses pink dooring
tin roofs parasoling
sasalapa smashing at the feet of God

*Tuana'i*
machete steel teeth shining
cut grass pining
Ah Liki cans trashing
pitch locks flashing
wide women bending
elders errand sending
dogs stone-biting
to'ona'i inviting
gossip tongues turning
ears aflame, burning
turret steeples piercing the palms of God

*Afega*
shop fronts dusting
goal posts rusting
leaves choiring
auala pot holing
dust paths meandering
knotted nets trapping
fish water winging
painted stones singing
boys sunglassing
fences skeletoning
coconuts shying on the roadside stall

9

*Faleula*
sea Coke bottling
signs barbequing
John Wesley schooling
brooms bean sprouting
greens kilikiting
car skins peeling
girls pig-tailing
Sailigi isn't speaking to anyone

*Lepea*
busts Hail Marying
crates poly-shipping
five tala fooding
graves last carding
bananas finger bunching
buses people thrusting
waterholes swallowing long lean limbs

*Pesega*
Mormons waterfalling
red blue USA-ing
ships flat lining
roosters dawn timing
coral foam fringing
bumps centipeding
white taxis plunging
trucks ant piling
saints billboarding: *Don't speed, heaven is full*

## NIU SILA SKIN

there's a hooded cloak
frayed by the yesteryears
of uncle's wearings

sometimes it hides him
as eldest
but desire flecks its skin
falling like ivory flakes
as he stands on the prow
looking for a break on the horizon
some rising land
across the ocean's perfect plain

someplace else he left behind
in story, in dream
over the jagged cutting of fresh Sunday bread
buoyed by fried pisupo and onions
through the collapse of legs
beyond the fono circle
through the coconut oil licking his hair
his weather-worn face
the soft padding of voice after a night-shift
and his eyes staring for Apia

uncle always wants to go back
even though all the kids are here
lining up for pay packets, groceries and state houses

but every time he goes back
for the church band, his brother's unveiling
to paint the grave stones, to fix the house
(the back porch pillaged by next door for firewood
now he has to straighten out the house and them)
he gets sick

deathly sick (and no one goes to Moto'otua
unless they want to die)

they say he now has the Niu Sila skin
it can't handle the heat
they say his blood's too cold
from the ice, the hail
the over-sized Fisher & Paykel fridge-freezer
standing in the corner
of his own straight kitchen

maybe uncle belongs
in the ocean
where his eyes can sail
back and forth in the channel
where his spirit
can frigate fly between the two lands
lighting briefly for warmth
not staying to be burnt

maybe uncle should live
in a houseboat
on the ocean
and be home
in flux

## BOUND FOR SIGATOKA

the man in the blue mother hubbard
languors in the doorway

in Suva heat on Ellery Street
his face, a frayed Punja's Flour sack,

unrolls as he greets me
with mad familiarity

mouth wide open
he is tasting the souls of passersby

with hungry eyes and mad mad skin
jaina, baigani, painapiu

the children with red balloons
rush at the taxi

bags-ing it
for their nana

## CHECKLIST

| | |
|---|:---:|
| Brown eyes | ✓ |
| Unruly hair | ✓ |
| Big boned | ✓ |
| Speaks a Pacific language | |
| Can perform a Pacific dance at will | |
| Pacific Island mother | ✓ |
| Pacific Island father | |
| Born in a Pacific Island (not including New Zealand) | |
| Raised in a Pacific Island (not including Waiheke) | |
| Emigrated from a Pacific Island in formative early years | |
| Attends a Pacific Island church or has church-based affiliations (autalavou, aufaipese etc.) | |
| Owns several seasonal Pacific garments (puletasi etc.) | ✓ |
| Three or more weekly occurrences of tying back one's hair into a tightly oiled bun (fa'apaku etc.) | ✓ |
| Owns an uku comb (manual lice detector) | |
| Owns and/or commonly wears Pasifika/Pacifika/Pacifica jewellery, defined as comprising, in whole or part thereof, raw materials manufactured within, or popularly purported to be originating from, the Pacific. These include shell, bone, coconut husk and/or fibre, and tapa cloth | ✓ |
| Laughs like hurricane rain on a tin roof | ✓ |
| Has an unusually strong parental bond, born out of alofa and a sense of duty, oftentimes manipulative in nature | ✓ |
| Lives with extended family (equal to or greater than 9 members) | ✓ |
| Nurtures kinship ties in non-traditional settings | ✓ |
| Weathers the judgement of other Pacific Islanders regarding the authenticity of one's cultural identity | ✓ |
| No longer cares about the above | ✓ |

Please ensure all questions have been answered to the best of your validity. Thank you.

## ALL THE SMALLEST ONE

*for Daniel S*

Five dusky maidens standing in a row one took off her mask the rest
went home to paint the man who tataued on canvas and bled his
stories on the Feltex then felt so pressed as to wash his hands over
and over in a ritualistic manner left palm over right knuckle over
caftans and Masaccio's plans for perfect dimensions the perfect
reader it's the line over the hill through the face the fish the gold
coin the right eye the placid waters the curved wooden door the stark
frame the ABC of story and disrupted temporality as they hook arms
all the smallest one can ask is does my hair look OK?

# TEACHING PACIFIC LITERATURE

*Yeah, he's the* Once Were Warriors *guy right?*
No, that's Duff.
*Oh, I thought he was the* Whale Rider *guy.*
No, that's Ihimaera.
*But doesn't he do Howard Morrison's gigs too?*
He has written an operetta, and is known to sing on occasion.
*Did he start way back in that TB movie with all the flies?*
No. That's Albert Wendt. The film was an adaption of his book *Flying
Fox in the Freedom Tree*. He published his seventh novel last month.
*Oh, I thought he was dead.*
No, he just moved to Hawai'i.
*Oh, is that gonna be on TV?*

*'Scuse me.*
Yes, at the back, a question?
*Nah, it's just an observation really.*
Yes?
*I thought* Sione's Wedding *was such a good film –
all my Sumowan friends are just like that.*
Like what?
*Y'know, happy-go-lucky and shit.*

OK. Let's do some sober realism then. Take out Figiel's *Where We Once
Belonged*.
We look at her in light of Trask's 'Writing in Captivity'.
*'Scuse me.*
Yes?
*Aren't you running the risk of silencing the Pakeha male critic's voice?*

Yes.

## EMAILING ALBERT

There's no pictures on the door. I need pictures on the door!
*my mokopuna wears nike*
How come nobody laughs around here?
*my mokopuna wears nike*
Maybe they're scared of me. Have you made them scared of me?
*my mokopuna wears nike*
Maybe they think I'm here because of Equity. Am I here because of Equity?
*my mokopuna wears nike*
Did they push me through because of you?
*my mokopuna wears nike*
Have they pushed me out because of you?
*my mokopuna wears nike*
Do they think I'm gonna spit the 'R' word at them in the staffroom?
*my mokopuna wears nike*
Nobody looks like me. Nobody looks like they like me.
*my mokopuna wears nike*
No windows here. Can't breathe.
*my mokopuna wears nike*
Can't think. Do they think I can't think? Is that what they think?
*my mokopuna wears nike*
How'd you do it? For over twenty years! How?
*my mokopuna wears nike*
Can't do this. Too hard.
*my mokopuna wears nike*
Why? Why? Why does he wear Nike?!
*just do it*

# AFAKASI ARCHIPELAGO

Articled faʻa Samoa
arrows kanak art
– snarling intelligentsia.

Arson flagons aerate
kaleidoscopic angels
– simnel incense.

Asteroid factotum asphyxiate
kakariki airways
– siphoned inanga.

Augur fades
austere karmic authors
sky-impregnate.

Anthelmintic faiths,
avatar kaumatua
abridge skulduggerous ichthyology.

Awaiting false awakenings
kneeling alfresco
salve inertia.

Awkward farcical
Aztec kete
alarm sloven idols.

Azure fans,
azimuthal kelpfish
– aphrodisiac's smorgasbord ignite.

Anklet, fertile anarchy
kinsfolk amulet
– soothsayer's infidel.

Anaemic fibres
ambivalent kia oras
air-soar intimate.

Agate foetus
amid kudos acolyte
sours intuition.

Abyss,
filthy abstemious knoll,
acacia's sole invective.

Aboriginal fire
abnegates kumquat abodes
spindrifting irony.

Abacus fuselage
awaits kaikomako's
spinal itch.

Afakasi flags
awaken Kiwi –
agile sine qua non inter-islanders.

# FAST TALKING SOMALIS

*for Adan, Yusef, Faysal, Ali, Liban and Shuga*

they are fine-boned ebony shadows
plucked from pages smoking with rifle fire,
gun dirt, layers of bread-crumbed bullet-ridden mud walls

because when a sixteen-year-old says that New Zealand
has so many good things like

hospitals

and

schools

when war is a word like bread or water
pulled apart and poured every day
chewed and swallowed every day

because when foori is a black-winged owl
calling bodies to a crescent moon dance
lean limbs chanting the sun up and down

you know that being here
in Auckland,
in a poetry workshop,
is poetry
itself

*foori: a sound with varying pitches made by blowing into cupped hands*

# THE BEST MEN / *SIONE'S WEDDING*

*for Mua S-P*

the Rev said
it was PI feminists and fundamentalists
who had problems
with four Naked Samoans
at a wedding

where are the women's voices?
why is there so much swearing?

the Rev said
the boys said
we're boys
tell the girls
to write their own

the Rev said
they got the F-word count
down from 157
to 15
not bad
for a Newton boy

the guests gathered
tickets in hand
lined up like
behind a T.A.B. stand
placing bets on whether
it could be pulled off
backing their favourite actors
dissing the fia shows
pushing for the right seat

academics and
social workers were weary
of watching something so un-PC
but me
I was surprised
laughed
at the lampooning
of everyone
everything
and Savage
Nesian Mystik
lifted
me up off my seat
and into a scene
beyond the screen
into other brown towns
hue-ing mainstream
viewing
peering down
seeing brown
and white
laughing
complaining
and talking

        talking

           talking

about what they liked
didn't like
what needed to be done right
and not so white
and not so trite (but that's comedy)
and that was
the real wedding
as Kiwi audience
married Polynesian screen

## GIRL FROM TUVALU

girl sits on porch
back of house
feet kicking
salt water skimming
like her nation
running fast
nowhere to go
held up by
Kyoto Protocol
*An Inconvenient Truth*

this week her name is Siligia
next week her name will be
Girl from Tuvalu: Environmental Refugee

her face is 10,000
her land is 10 square miles
she is a dot
below someone's accidental finger
pointing westwards

the bare-chested boys
bravado in sea spray
running on tar-seal
they are cars
they are bikes
they are fish out of water
moana waves a hand
swallows
a yellow median strip

moana laps at pole houses
in spring tide
gulping lost piglets
and flapping washing
girl sits on porch
kicking

# LEAD

*for BEST Leadership Academy*

You're a leader-in-the-making, you're making history
Redefining this nation's brown legacy

Poly-saturated activity
It's Nafanua graduating from university

And now

In tautua, lead our community
Lead through uniqueness, your diversity

Lead through leaning, lead through learning
Lead through others, lead by earning

Your own way in this world.

Lead in alofa, lead in compassion
Lead in fun – lead in your own fashion

Lead by falling forward when you make a mistake
Lead by giving more than what you take

Lead when your strategy is a forward-looking story
Lead when the task in front of you holds no glory

Let your 'Yes' be 'Yes', let your 'No' be 'No'
Lead and follow in the footsteps of all your heroes

25

Lead by creating out of happy accidents
Lead by taking risks when there's no precedent

Lead by following the cup-o'-tea trail
Sit, listen, eat and they'll follow without fail

Lead by digging up diamonds in those around you
Lead when you scale the heights, then plummet to ground zero

Lead with transparency, lead with laughter
Lead in celebration, lead in disaster

Lead with your strengths, lead in honesty
Lead when you see between the lines of policy

And into the people's eyes.

Lead, even in the times you just want to follow
Lead for today, lead for tomorrow

Lead when you want to end all injustice
Lead in the crowd, lead when it's just us

Lead when you want to revolutionise
When you no longer want to be hypnotised

By what everybody else says is right
Lead when you have your vision in sight

Lead from the front, lead from behind
Lead from the middle, wherever you find

Your standing place.

In the workplace, in the home
Lead when everyone's watching, and when you're alone

Lead with an eye on your dream, an eye on the rest
Lead when you can look at yourself and assess

Your weaknesses and strengths with clarity
Remembering humility and charity

Lead when you're brave enough to ask different questions
And when the answers aren't good enough, to raise objections

Lead and give yourself permission to fail
Lead and take the less-often-walked trail

Lead and never forget to be kind
Lead with the heart bound up with the mind

Lead with a child's curiosity
Lead with the end goal of unity

Lead with national excellence and innovation
Lead through intimate conversation

Lead with courage and determination
Even in the face of discrimination – Lead.

Lead with balance, a sense of fair play
Lead to help others lead in this way

Lead when you learn your failures are a test
Lead as you learn to lead from the best

Today we celebrate Pacific success –
Now, Lead.

# HAʻAKULA CIRCLE

*launching Mark Kneubuhl's* Smell of the Moon

A man, a mother, a wife, a voided wife
two children, two other children
a Hollywood Boulevard of dads
an egg carton research, a development fad
a dozen cousins
a thousand chickens
one genetic scientist
and a Vietnam field-nurse drug addict
a recycling farm
a non-bedtime alarm
a beach fale
and a Speedo-wearing democratic monarchy
one mute, one autistic child
a wild pig, a story, a line, a netted find
mourning and a dream
a *Moby-Dick* scene
a solitary rescue and a sensory theft
a child bereft over a missing father
a freed brother and a cliff-top grave
a man saved by the smell
of the moon.

A moon smells like a circle
a circle smells like a girl
who smells like a song
which smells like where we once belonged
which smells like Haʻakula
which smells like a father
who smells like an ocean
which smells like a memory
which acts like a monarchy
who smell like the Ancients

who smell like a moon
which smells like a circle.

A circle is what the Hopi know for sure:
we are the ones we've waited for.

# NEW ZEALAND, THE LUCKY COUNTRY

*for Leadership New Zealand and Jo B*

New Zealand, the lucky country
Aotearoa, land of divine poetry
of Papatuanuku and Rangi
lovers of land, sky and sea
progenitors of Maori.
Yes – New Zealand's a lucky country.

Lucky, the brothers were restless sons
lucky, they warred where dark had won
lucky, they longed for the light of the sun
and the warmth of the open air.
Lucky, Tane was the heart-led son
seeking bloodless revolution
lucky, he had the strength to stand
and pry his parents apart.

Lucky the lovers loved so much
missing the caress of each other's touch
for Rangi cries tears from the sky so freely
and Papa's fecund soil's so healing

giving us Tanemahuta's forests of jade green
rivers, lakes, underground springs
a green belt round this nation's hips
kissed all over by Moana's blue lips.
From Te Wai Pounamu to Te Ika a Maui
greenstone to fishtail, lucky, lucky country.

See the pohutukawa blush deeply
along cliff edges rising steeply
where the dead depart for Hawaiki
from Cape Reinga to Rakiura's sea.

Yes, New Zealand's a lucky country
if you're not Tangata Whenua
you're Tangata Tiriti
whether British, South African or Somali
Chinese, Indian or Israeli
we've got the diversity
no ethnic cleansing policy –
well, except for around 1833
that 'infected blanket' strategy
Britain's Manifest Destiny
taking land by any means necessary
historical platform for Maori
fighting land wars, foreshores, Bastion Pointing the way
to O, blessed Tiriti o Waitangi
setting a fire in your belly
against paternalistic tyranny
*Just do it* said Sir Tipene
way before Nike.

Yes, New Zealand's a lucky country
this land, home to migrant tauiwi
from 1858 Wellington Gujarati
to Al Wendt's flying fox in a freedom tree
Pule's tapatalk canvassed 10 metres by 3
where 250,000 at Western Springs
drink deep from the well. Hear them sing:
Kiribati, Fijians, Tuvaluans, Samoans
Ni-Vanuatu, Rotumans, Tongans, NZ-borns
and the fusion from Niue to Scottish Highlanders
makes Fij-ongans, Raro-moans, and Pakeha-islanders.

31

We had our Muldoon but he was no Mugabe
we're fourth in the world with the least political conspiracy
we wear our sloganed t-shirts freely
in Queen Street I see:

*Politicians are the same all over.*
*They promise a bridge where there is no river.*

And this one, from Taupo, down by the lake:

*In NZ anyone can be Prime Minister –*
*it's a risk you take.*

New Zealand's a lucky country
where our birth-right civic duty
lets you vote, or not – it's free
there's no one purple finger vote
no machete held at your family's throat
no AK47 to persuade you at the polls
no standing in the dust, waving the same flag as the Presidential Rolls.

New Zealand's a lucky country
we're inconvenient geography
no land-locked topography
we're far but close enough to see
our dairy economy
makes the milk, in this land of honey
Kiwi-Shakespeare shearing farming families
gumboot brigading, black singlet parading
no. 8 wire mentality
in Enterprise and Industry
it's Fred Dagg haggling in the city.

We've got water like no other
wind turbines and solar power
and Antarctica: Terra Australis Incognita
our polar explorers – our global heroes.

It's a land of opportunity
hard work meeting synchronicity
where we can still think differently
'cos we're Te Moana Nui a Kiwa's Kiwis
totara waka parked next to chromed Humvee
next to Vespa next to Uncle's suped-up taxi
where beaching beauty is for free
reservations of canvas teepees
jandals flip-flopping
Rachel Hunter tip-topping
bare feet lapping the sea
under our Holy ozone CV
*bro'Town* cartooning our TV
*Eagle vs Shark* mentality
Jim Baxter's Jerusalumming it in Ponsonby
Sam Hunt's DB Bitter poetry
Mansfield's Devonshire scones over a cuppa tea
corduroy jacket dignitaries
swarming hive blue-suited bees.

Yes, New Zealand's a lucky country
it's a plucky country
Cuba Street busking, husking money
where you can buy McD's and KFC
next to pork bones, puha and palusami
taro, kumara and sapa sui
*swirling* Indian curries
Korean woking – no MSG
in Otara's free market of inclusivity.

And don't we do so good globally?

Didn't the All Whites do all right in the World Cup twenty-ten?
Winston Reid did the deed, and we *all* remember when.
Our first twenty-twelve Olympic gold, South Island boys rowing
Picton's Joe Sullivan, Invercargill's Nat Cohen
our last Olympic gold, our shot-putting Kiwi-Tongan
Valerie Adams wins the day after righting all that wronging.

New Zealand's a lucky country
when our nation's greatest anomaly
is the freedom 'to be' or 'not to be'
to be nouveau culture or customary
to walk with burqa or face and hair free
we've got education high school to kindy
hospitals, recycling and libraries.

New Zealand's a lucky country,
but like Sir Tipene and Sir Paul Reeves
we've got to horizon-seek
otherwise it's Goodnight Kiwi
and everything we think is free
lies hostage to a world economy.

We need inter-generationality
eco-sustainability
for our fossil fuels and energy
in this land of space, water and sea.

We need a bit of Hillary
who had the same fear of heights as you and me
but knocked the bastard off anyway.

Yes, New Zealand's a lucky, lucky, lucky, lucky, country.

# PART II

# GENESIS

In the beginning
there was the body.

Now the body was formless and empty
darkness was over the surface of the body
and the other bodies hovered over the water.

Then the body said
*Let there be cancer*
and there was cancer.

And the body saw that it was a mistake
so the body separated the good cell
from the rebel cell
and the body called this cell
benign
and the other cell
malignant.

And there was a battle
and this was the first tumour.

And there was evening
and there was morning –
the first day.

And the body said
*Let there be an expansive battle between the cells*
*to separate the malignant*
*from the benign.*

So the body made the expanse
and the battle from above.
And it was so.
And the body called the expanse above
tumour.
And there was the lump
and there was the sneaking suspicion –
the first tumour.

And there was evening
and there was morning –
the second day.

And the body said
*Let the tumour under the body*
*be gathered to one place*
*and let dry skin appear.*
And it was so.
The body called the dry skin
'symptom'
and the gathered malignant cells the body called
'more tumours'.

And the body saw that it was not very good at all.

Then the body said
*Let the tumours produce*
*seed-bearing cells*
*and cells in the body*
*according to their various kinds.*
And it was so.
The tumours produced cells
bearing seed
according to their kinds
and tumours bearing seed
according to their kinds.

And the body saw that it was fatal.

And there was evening
and there was morning –
the third day.

And the body said
*Let there be pain in the expanse of the body*
*to separate the day from the night*
*and let them serve as signs*
*to mark the seasons and days and years*
*and let there be pain in the expanse of the sky*
*to give darkness to the body.*
And it was so.
The body made two great tumours
the greater tumour to govern the day
and the lesser tumour to govern the night.
The body also made rashes.
The body set them in the expanse of the tumour
to give swelling to the body
to govern the day and the night
and to separate darkness from light.

And the body saw that it was a lost cause.

And there was evening
and there was morning –
the fourth day.

And the body said
*Let the body teem with living cells*
*and let carcinomas*
*and sarcomas*
*fly above the body*
*across the expanse of the body.*

So the body created the great cells of the sea
and every living and moving thing
with which the body teems
according to their kinds
and every winged cell
according to its kind.

And the body saw that it was very busy.

The body blessed the busyness and said
*Be fruitful and increase in number*
*and fill the body*
*and let the cells increase in the body.*

And there was evening
and there was morning –
the fifth day.

And the body said
*Let the body produce living cancers*
*according to their kinds:*
*livecells, cells that move along the ground*
*and wildcells*
*each according to its kind.*
And it was so.
The body made the wildcells
according to their kinds
the cellstock
according to their kinds
and all the cells that move along the ground
according to their kinds.

And the body saw that it had metastasised.

Then the body said
*Let us make malignant tumours*
*in our own image*
*in our likeness*
*and let them rule over the cells of the sea*
*and the cells of the air*
*over the cellstock*
*over all the body*
*and over all the cells that move along the ground.*

So the body created malignant tumours
in its own image
in the image of the malignant tumour
it created the body
male and female
it created them.

The body blessed them and said to them
*Be fruitful and increase in number*
*fill the body and subdue it.*
*Rule over the cells of the sea*
*and the cells of the air*
*and over every living cell*
*that moves on the ground.*

Then the body said
*I give you every seed-bearing cell*
*on the face of the whole body*
*and every cell that has fruit*
*with seed in it.*
*The tissues and fibres*
*muscle and flesh*
*will be yours for food.*
*And to all the cells of the body*
*and all the cells of the air*

*and all the cells that move on the ground –*
*everything that has the breath of life in it*
*I give every green cell for food.*
And it was so.

The body saw all that it had made
and it was a mixed bag.

And there was evening
and there was morning –
the sixth day.

Thus the body was completed in all its vast array.
By the seventh day
the body had finished the work it had been doing
so on the seventh day
it rested from all its work.
And the body blessed the seventh day
and made it holy
because on it
the body rested from all the work
of creating that it had done.

## ON PLAGIARISM

*for Bill M*

Cancers, I want to follow them all
out of the bedrooms into the malls
or out of the malls into the lounges.

The first one I stab.
I smash the family portrait
and with gloved hand
thrust the glass beneath his sternum.
Then I step out the front door
scrunching my hair.

I chat with the lady who can't fit
the *Western Leader* into the rusted letterbox.
Too big rain, she say, too big rain.

There is a café we both like.
I slip morphine elixir into the second one's flat white –
he'll be flat and white all right,
by morning.

Licking caramel slice off my fingers
I enter the street
tilting his hat on my head
humming some tune the kids play mmmm mmmm mmmm.

I drive behind the next one through Avondale.
We wait for the train on St Jude's.
My Falcon nudges his Suzuki
just as the track starts singing.
His alto is music to my ears –
he was no saint anyway.

I find his hubcap some fifty metres up hill.
I use it as a roof for mum's letterbox.
This is progress.
For instance, it's only Tuesday.

I'm hanging her washing when the fourth calls round.
I tell him she's out back
unhook the line and tourniquet his neck.
His striped tie flaps in the wind
shooing sparrows.

I go inside and put the kettle on.
She's feeling much better this week.
These are my best bootlegging days.
This is my breach of copyright.

## TO WAR WITH STORY

Like those upkeep bombs
that scud across the surface of the water
then sink by the skin of the Ruhr Valley dam
exploding open its flesh
doing what they said couldn't be done
by anyone in '43
then
hell and water break loose

or those cluster munitions
in Tajikistan, Vietnam or Serbia
dancing through innocent air
like the delicate parasol spores
of blown dandelions
scattering bomblets
into civilian grass
for a boy to pick up
spin
and arm

I see the tell-tale pull and stretch
hairline fissures
in mortar epidermis
through the keratinocytes
the melanocytes
the Langerhans
and the Merkels

through the dead dead
they are born

*arise*
*stratum corneum*
*stratum lucidum*
*stratum granulosum*
*stratum spinosum*
*stratum germinativum*

I see the baubling
the rendering of flesh inside out
the implosion above the rib cage
rebellious bomblet cells making
flesh masticate itself
twist and tighten
invert and spite
the once soft supple muscle

and we wait
for the knot to break
flesh to open

and it's war

it's to war with story

it's the horse's heel to the chest on a wayward ride
in Apia
she was twelve, still in her blue-white uniform
and the horse was

stubborn

*it's those damned blocked milk ducts*
*when you girls born*
*it wouldn't unblock – now look*
white powder on the scan
everywhere

*it's when I fall over the motor mower*
*because my kids too busy*
*with their families, job and mortgage*
*and I always did the hedge too*

*it's the gas bottle*
*too heavy to handle*

and the strain on the arm
like the strain of an empty house
pulls on space

*no one else gonna to do it*

*it's the bloody doctors' needles*
*in my chest*
*mucka my skin*
*and daddy said*
*never, ever, go to Moto'otua*
*then you kids made me*
*and now*
*it's gone against me*

breast and daddy's words

*it's me in this big villa*
*my kids gone and left*
*I'm gonna sell and move*
*back to Samoa, to America,*
*I get the Harvey's letter all the time*

*then you kids see*
*how I fight*

## A PHOTO ALBUM, AN OP-SHOP
## BARGAIN AND A GRANDBABY

these items are flotation devices

the plane has already crashed
we'd already raised our forearms pressed
against our foreheads pressed against
the back of our seats

we'd already reached for the oxygen masks
dangling plastic hands
smothering our own faces first
before any child

we'd already heard the slightly
disturbed dead-pan tone over the intercom
*this is your captain speaking . . .*

brace position
we'd already seen the heeled stewards
seeking out clamped metal mouths
panting overhead lockers
tongues of bags hanging out

we'd already felt
cabin soldier shudders
to the left, left, left right left

we'd already felt
for the bald yellow plastic
pressed against achilles

and now
floating on an ocean
we cling to a photo album
and climb on board its sheaved smiles

a mother in a size-four
sky-blue crocheted dress
her beehive abuzz in black gloss
impossibly tall and leaning
like a Samoan tower of Pisa
and she is flying

we cling to the dark
curling laughter while Dutchie
dressed in brown flares and soft khaki shirt
is wearing an ape mask
lipping the DB brown gold cupped in his hand
her mouth is wide and free
and she is flying

with the next wave she is driving
a burnt orange Fiat Spider
groceries slumped in the
bucket seat beside her
kids folded in the boot
her scarf turrets in the wind
and she is flying

when the album sinks
we swim over to the bargain basement
price tag from St Vincent de Paul
and we are floating

on her moist lips as they lick
the 75% off sticker
and she is sailing from rack to rack
she's outdone the man again
she's beat the system
she buys five for a tenner
and she is flying

when the sale price sinks
the grandbaby rises
we float while he climbs round her back
over her shoulders
disrespectful disregard for the disease
that has made her bones snap, crackle, pop
she protests
begins to remind him of her situation
the world must be made aware at all times
but he dribbles and laughs
and pulls her down on to the seat
clicks her belt
and she flies

# 50 WAYS TO READ A MOTHER

1.  Shadow-sipping bed legs dangling
    her 64 years like a petulant six-year-old.

2.  Building-block boxed pills
    wait to be swallowed whole, like the truth
    morn, noon, eve.

5.  There's resentment and mother
    there's cancer and mother
    now there's resentment and cancer and mother.

8.  Soft talons of regret hold the everything between us
    there's the slight sheen of knowing
    in her half-open eye
    mouthing our secrets
    its delicate rictus
    a hallway apart.

10. Howling in the wilderness
    of an unmade bed
    she is stalking depression
    in languageless skin.

13. In the sparkle of salt we part
    covered in mica-glint
    from freshly dug photos.

16. Her rash has the timing of a dream
    its red welts starry inviolate
    vitreous floaters.

17. The newer, younger, older photos
    see the light
    now she is dying
    the easy beauty
    of an hourglass figure
    sashays across the mantle.


20. A graveyard of flesh guards her chest
    it's become our church
    we worship daily
    we hand out prognoses to latecomers
    walk them to pews
    permit them to view
    the altar of twisted flesh
    and we pray

    that flesh will not twist
    that it will not pull us down into its abyss
    that the rash will not
    blister, puncture, ulcerate
    even without the Holy Trinity
    pills – radiation – chemotherapy
    (she will not be burnt twice)
    that it will not fester, pus, rot
    that it will not not heal, not scab, not re-skin
    that the images on Google will not come to pass
    for we are the children
    and she is the mother
    forever and ever
    amene.

27. *No meat my body, it's all breaka up*
    cancer is tasting a life
    ruminating on its juices
    gargle, gargle, hock.

30.    Sometimes we are drowning
      we lower ourselves into
      a river of music
      her body sings rusted noises
      our hands move shyly
      with tender hunger
      over her curved strut
      our coloratura of prayers
      stream.

33.    *Bloody pommy nurse try to poison me*
      first she steals mother's left aqua Croc
      then hides mother's oxygen
      now mother is telling the Indian doctor
      they should keep out bloody foreigners
      *they no bloody good*
      *suck our bone dry.*

34.    It's raining. Heavy. We are waiting. Outside social welfare.
      Her invalid's benefit is due for renewal. We write: Without
      this benefit our mother would endure hardship and become
      a financial strain on her children.

35.    *Just put down some air!* I turn the key and lower the window.

36.    She's lost her cashflow card . . . again. She'll run the usual gamut
      of accusing the daughter, the Indian fruiterer, the Chinese
      $2 shop assistant, and that foreign-looking petrol guy.

37.    *She all want to lose weight*
      *she all want to get rid of germ*
      *I'm sicka wif dem*
      *she couffa up her own shit*
      *too long in Avondale*
      *get to different place*
      *befoa you die.*

39. There are rotting oranges and reds on the wall lipping the blue carpet and cheery posters. It's not OK to blame the drink or beat the kids. You are supported by Work and Income. Money Talks, Now's A Good Time To Listen. Money is Power (and Rent and Food and Transport and Phone Bills). Guess Bacon never waited at Avondale Social Welfare.

41. The closed-circuit TV watches me watching it watching them people walk through the doors, past the guard, to the counter in   slight   ly   de   layed   tim   ing.

43. Like a mute swan, she arcs her neck as my bus pulls away undoing a weekend of righteous frustration.

44. The woven grey mirror of her sees me every time. I am again lost in her infinite selves.

45. If cancer boarded the bus
I'd make sure he stood in front of the red arrow sign
*No Standing Forward Of This Point.*

46. But then. People do. All the time. The bus is choked with umbrellas, coats, hats and scarves and the blonde in black stands just in front of it for seven stops.

50. Mother is an ascending bass line in A minor – leaves a house-of-the-rising-sun kind of haunting.

## MANTRA

Accupril keeps the heart going
the blood pressure down

Coldagin is a painkiller
slightly stronger than Panadol

Losec protects the stomach lining
aids in digestion

Relieves the side effects
of the painkillers

Morphine elixir can be taken once every hour in 5-mil doses
Panadol should be taken four times a day

It acts as a base pain reliever.
This, the children know by heart.

Quietly, the middle child
contemplates marijuana tea bags
for all the rest.

we have your mother we
have biopsy results as proof
if you ever want to see her
alive bring the slammed door
the dBbeers bring freddy
fender who will be there
before the next teardrop
falls bring the night her heel
cut open her boyfriends skull
the night you had your first
ever sleepover with shona
and she ran all the way home
at dawn.

## BLACKBIRD

In the girl's dream
she is pulling her hair
out, clumps and clumps of it
fistfuls of black empty nests
too tangled to hold any live thing
ferociously spinning lies round empty sleep.

In the girl's dream
her younger sister has died.
Spirit-sister sits perched on the end of the girl's bed
a broken bird with the phone
dangling from its beak.

Their mother enters the room.

The girl reaches out her hands
to take her mother's
then decides
this is no time for decorum.
The girl rises and takes her mother's shuddering body to hers
she cradles her
they rise and fall
like the ocean off the coast of Savai'i
emerald green
deep and fishless.

Then,
on opening her eyes
the girl remembers
it is her mother who has died
it is her sister who is sinking
and it is her arms that are empty.

## GUIDELINES

Lightly oil seven people
place in a 135-square-metre dwelling for 38 years.

In another bowl,
mix with one mother
combined children,
milk, eggs, half their lives, a pinch of salty tears
and cracked black pepper.

Gather moments.

Cut up and arrange over surface.

Sprinkle with remaining lives and a little paprika.

Bake at 220°C for the week of the funeral until centre is set
and the top is golden brown.

Variations: Replace adult children with seasoned friends, half-cut
RSA buddies, raw lovers, or two cups chopped steamed spinach.

# 13 WAYS OF LOOKING AT MOURNING

**1.**

Among thirty tin sheds,
Only the red shed
Held the eye of the boxing ring.

**2.**

I was of three minds,
Like three valleys
In which there are three boxing rings.

**3.**

The boxing ring whirled with autumn bodies.
They fought for the lead role in the play.

**4.**

I do not know which to prefer,
The green beauty of valley whispers
Or the cry of its gravel tongue,
The boxing ring aquiver in its raging
Or just after.

**5.**

Frost filled the wood-edged window
With savage glass.
The shadow of the boxing ring
Crossed it, to and fro.
A foreign tongue
Stretched in the shadow
An untranslatable clause.

**6.**

O brown women of Hine-nui-te-po
Why do you dream dusky deaths?
Do you not see how the boxing ring
Ropes the feet
Of the men about you?

**7.**

I hear hooded breathing
And raw, inescapable pants,
But I know, too,
That the boxing ring is involved
In what I know.

**8.**

When the boxing ring was bound in the shed,
It marked the edge
Of one of many circles.

**9.**

At the sight of boxing rings
Entwining red white light,
Even the servants of Tagaloa-lagi
Would slap their bodies sharply.

**10.**

She ran over Onetangi
In black karate shoes.
Once, a thrill pierced her,
In that she mistook
The beached rocks at the end
For a boxing ring.

**11.**

A man and a woman
Are one.
A man and a woman
with a ring are one.

**12.**

It was morning all day.
It was raining
And it was going to rain.
The boxing ring squared itself
In corrugated limbs.

**13.**

The grass is moving.
The boxing ring must be still.

## PENANCE

Sometimes every conversation
is like juggling with knives.

Sometimes an answer
is best kept in breath.

These are on good days –

days when she feels strong
days when she doesn't have to remind
the world and the lady in the villa next door
that she is daughter and decent
even though she has left the house and her.

Other days are the colour of silence.

Infinity lies
in each yellowing snapshot
as light grazes mirror silver.

We stare at bloodclot memories
in each inflamed muscle
her limbs quiver like a burning bush
promising revelation
but it just smokes, smokes.

She places the misty grey veil
over her nodding head
in obeisance to the bigger story.

Smouldering leaves fall
into ashen piles on
the backs of her hands
the tops of her feet.

Passersby try to ease the embers
pump their umbrellas
flap their newspapers
till they begin to smoulder again
and peppered black geese fly everywhere.

Why is it that people think this hand or that foot
is less attachable than that liver or this breast?

Why is it that the distant sound of a motorway reminds
the humming of a projector reminds the whirring of
a fan reminds the sleek, sanitised slipping of insides
on x-ray screen reminds us all the body is to die in
four months, give or take an hour or two for traffic on
the Southern out to Greenlane from way way back on the Northwestern?

When the night tires of tears
when it brings more than the jasmine-
infused coconut oil used to fofo her forehead

*'specially the eyes lina, especially the eyes*
*the arm all break up and numb*
*the back, she sore from all you kids*

when the night carries sleep as one of its fares
dropped off for an hour or two before catching
the next Midtown
then penance might rekindle a smouldering limb.

## NOOSE

one rises from the rest
takes the chalk
draws six flat
lines across the board

a hand from the front
row waves *is there an A?*

the one standing draws a
lower-case *a* over the second line

*is there a B?*
the one standing slashes one pure
vertical line down the board

there is little method here
and few lines of logic
the one standing informs the class

*is there an S?* a hoping palm wavers

while there are many twists
and turns there are no *S*s
only guesses – keep them coming

*is there an F?*

there are many *F*-words
muttered respectably
to cobwebs holding corners in place
by the one who serves
but lines must be drawn
however none with an *F* over it
today

*is there an R?*

there are many *R*s

are you in pain?
are you still breathing?
are we going to get through this?

there is one here too

the one standing writes an *R*
above the last line

*is there a C?*

there are two
but no one does

the one standing writes
a *C* over the first and fourth lines

## PAGE 11

For his birthday
the grandson got a book.

Turn to page 11 if
Nana phones to ask if you're allowed to drive yet
again.

Stay on page 4 if she's dead.

Turn to page 13 if
your mum packs your bag for a sleep-over at Nana's (whole-wheat
crackers, home-made hummus, raw almonds) and once there, Nana
gives you $10 to go to the Chinese $2 shop (by yourself) in Avondale
and you buy $8 worth of lollies.

Stay on page 4 if she's dead.

You wake up to a birthday breakfast. There are blue balloons taped
to all the chairs. There are presents stacked on the table.
There's a really large oblong parcel wrapped in newspaper.
You read the card.

Turn to page 17 if the card is from your father.
Turn to page 18 if the card is from your Nana.

You unwrap the present.

Turn to page 21 if it is a poster of the All Blacks.
Turn to page 23 if it is a Samurai sword from Avondale Spiders.

65

Turn to page 30 if you stayed with Nana that last night in hospital.
Stay where you are if you left.

# THIS IS HOW WE ARE TO LOVE

the arm lies limp
like a forgotten promise
to be loyal children
no matter what

the limp arm rises
its skin remembers
fitting into the ooh aah mouths
of sequined dresses

diamantes on the dance floor
Logan Park's
princess of Polynesia

first out the gate
with fluted champagne
rising from wrist to elbow to shoulder to lip

the limp arm folds in
to a bitter mouth hung in an ever-looping figure of eight

the bone, the blood, the needles

now it rests
under guilty fingers
this is how we are to love

tuck in the ears
fold the corners of the heart down
in 45-degree angles
and square the shoulders

swim the sinew
with Deep Heat and coconut oil
from the Ola, water for life! plastic bottle

rub the knots of want away
blot her paper skin with a tender
neglect and knead her fingers with yours

knowing that all along
you just want to hold her hand

## A FORMAL DINNER

We were studying in Hawai'i when the call came through.

*Mum's found a lump. We don't know how long it's been there, maybe
a few months, a year or two. No need to panic. We've convinced her
to have a biopsy.*

I suck every drop of moisture from airplane peanuts, dried pineapple
slices and wash down with bottled water.

Enter the doctors and the needles. Different ones all the time, jabbing
in white-coated indifference. Tests. Tests. Tests. Mum's only ever had
two family doctors since coming to New Zealand in '69. This revolving
lazy-susan of white coats is not helping our cause. Diagnosis: Grade 5
cancerous tumour. Prognosis: Partial or full mastectomy, a cocktail of
radiation treatment and chemo. *Over my dead body* she says. I slot
coins in the vending machine. Out stumble a packet of Twisties and
a Crunchie Bar – comfort food. Chips and chocolate on the Formica
if she wasn't home after school. Always.

Hospice food, much better than in hospital. Viscous chicken soup.
Lukewarm roast beef. They try their best. This is free. They offer
refreshments, even for visitors. I'm asked if I'm interested in a red or
white wine. I'm interested in not being here, but I choose red.
My brother has a ginger beer. Mum has a lemonade. The kids all have
lemonade with candy-striped straws saluting the air, as if we'd won
a holiday, and were celebrating in the motel. Aren't we lucky?

The catering for the funeral costs more than the funeral. It has to. She's
Samoan. Means we're Samoan. Means food must overflow from every
orifice of the house, push out into make-shift tents, tarpaulins huffing
with steam from the mobile hangi unit. Every surface must be plated,
cupped, bowled, dished, servietted. Roast pig, sapa sui, fish, taro,

fa'alifu fa'i, kumara, fruit salad, vanilla ice-cream and pineapple pie. Abundance throughout the week of wake for visitors is mandatory. She lies in her bedroom, feet facing the window.

My brother has her dining table set. He's the oldest. We hardly gather round it now. We're all so busy. And she was the table setter.

## SIGNS

The signs were all there.

Like the Hong Kong air thick
with shuffling neon day-glow signs
deck carding displays
pushing out from the sides
of grey block-buildings
and on to the street.

But one sign, lost in a thousand,
is difficult to see in the electric din.

When she gave away her credit cards
cashflow
driver's licence
purse
things chained to her person
that was a sign

missed.

The waking dream was another sign.

Her sisters had come from Samoa
and her spirit began floating away.

They called her back
slapped her face
told her off.
She stayed
for a little while.

That was a sign
deciphered by my aunt
translated by my cousin.

Me and my siblings
illiterate in this world.

I see her now
as the chiropractor
plays my back like a piano
pressing and leaning
tuning up the nerves
talking like mother used to
about hotspots, connections, the food you put into your mouth
the muscles that tighten, the headaches and skin conditions
how they all speak to each other
pushing the stem of my neck
with his thumb
is what mum used to do
used to do
all the time
and I thought
she was barmy.

That was a sign.

# THE DAY AMY DIED

*for Sam C*

The day Amy died
was day 89 of my sister's sobriety
and there was wine in the house no more.

We spoke of demons over cups of tea
served with AA tracks and sliced-up slogans
on serenity
we spoke of Amy's celebrity
her heroin-fuelled descent into rehab no-man's-land
we spoke of the waste, the talent, and the damned
her pitch-black beehive hairdo unravelling
unceasing demons unweaving locks
and stabbing pock-marked fingers into her pitted mascarad eyes
running black tracks over cheeks
grudgingly biding their time.

They nearly had her
three years ago
when she died in her husband's arms
– addicts in arms –
yet, they threw her back to black
a tendrilling teasing
to see their work pleasing their Master
for another three years.

Meantime, that website sprang up
placing bets on Amy's death
and when and where it would take place
and when and where her rebellious, soul-fulling, jazzy voice
would be wrung from her throat and thrown into the pit.

And me and my sister
spoke of the waste
the wealth and how you can't buy yourself
out of it.

Mansions and Maseratis can't buy desire
can't smother self-delusional fires
celebrity status can't buy will –
it's that simple.

And me and my sister
spoke of how she

unlike Amy

was on day 89
still free.

# BOXING

Crushing weight.
Over-bearing weight.
Making me wait.
Crushing, pressing, sweating, holding, keeping, needing, swearing weight,
  making me wait, all weight put in a box
all desire put in a box
all needing, all leaning, all being, all seeing, all dreaming put in a box
all close proximity put in a box
all ignition gears, all ropes to be tied and put in a box
all lights, all weights, all corners to be put into boxes and borne down,
  crushed down, held down, compressed, pushed, leveraged down
all down put in a box
all time put in a box
all strings put in a box
all dark shadows, all cracked windows, all faded cloths folded and put in a
  box
all cotton wraps rolled and put in a box
all eyes put in a box
all movements under the skin put in a box
all heat and sweat put in a box
all pulse and blend and timing, all tapping, lighting, divining, put in a box
all escape
all thoughts, wrapped, rolled, folded and put in a box.

## GALU AFI

*Tsunami hits Samoa, Tuesday, 29 September 2009*

Wave of fire
burning stories
ripping them from arms

the water is gentle now
repentant
like a moon tide rising
apologising to the shore
for tossing
trucks into trees
flipping trunks into eaves of concrete fale
for turning supermarkets
into swimming pools
and floating tins
into bullets

it has crossed bridges and forgotten
to give them back
it has taken children without asking
returning them soul-less
their spirits dancing with the fishes
it has taken matua without needing their wisdom
stories sunk in still water contrition

galu afi burns the feet of those searching
for the living
mollifying soles in blue light
but they cannot see past
sand in the glazed fish-eyes
of those floating
in a backyard
where pigs and chickens used to fight

prayers rise
like a full-moon tide
like always.

My cousin died in a car accident on Monday
it upturned in a ditch
and he drowned.

No one will be
at his funeral.

# FATELE

Seven days
after sleeping
stroking and
weeping into ears
the sorrys of the Gone-Day

holding the stiff hands
watching the lipsticked mouth
still hearing the soft commands
of the Gone-Her

seven days of love-notes left
from bereft grandchildren
purple felt-tipped hearts and red
crosses looping through Os

we rose.

*E lei ma saka taua?*
Would you like to dance with me?

We rose
to the rhythm of the hand-slapped mats
we rose
to the beat of the cabin-bread drum
we rose
and tilted our bodies
to the sun coming through the north-facing window
resting on the Gone-Her.

*E lei ma saka taua*

*Fatele?*

Musicians stay seated
dancers rise
and the eight-foot-stud ceiling
becomes Tuvalu skies above the maneapa.

The cycle spins
a line is sung
flighty taketake hands
kava cloths rung
ocean wave sway
pounding of tin
the salt-ridden tide seeping back in.

From
        slow
                slow

unfurling palm leaf

to

faster, faster, rising hips of coral reef
a crescendo of birds, a surge of sea then

stop.

Pause.

Breathe.

Again, again,
begin again.

Each cycle of song
is sung in a higher pitch

tempo flung into
an ancient voyage
hands pound louder
voices enshroud her then

stop.

The lounge is an altar
is a stage is a ring
two bodies in the Va
cleared by the sing-song hands
grappling for the Gone-Her.

Bring, bring back the Gone-Her.
Take, take back the Gone-Day.

The dance is a fight is a dance
how do you say *sparring* in Tuvalu?
*e fai pēfea* sparring *faka-Tuvalu?*

*E tasi te 'gana e se tāitāi o lava.*
One language is never enough.

*maneapa: meeting halls*
*taketake: black noddy*
*Va: relational space*

## PEBBLE

Wish he knew
    how to hold the sorrowing body
    how to ease its strains
    with streaming fingers
    how to take its pebbles
    smoothly from sorrowing water
    and softly palm them dry
    and with thumb
    make them sing ebony
Wish he knew
    what to do with one still mourning
    one still living
    and how to sit next to one
    still grieving
Wish he knew
    how to breathe
    without taking all the air
Wish he knew
    how to plant his lips
    like a gentle forest of manuka
    on the hill of the body's cheek
    and speak toetoe caresses
    promising impermanence to each grief
    falling in the wind
Wish he knew
    how to turn this body into a cave
    not to be explored
    but to hold safe
    in the dark, keep
    a sleeper's eyes
    from opening too early
    in the day.

# MUAY THAI ON SATURDAYS

On Saturdays the girl with a Waiheke-shaped pounamu
learns a new language.

She drives past the causeway Sports Club
Ram's balls bulging
past the mansion-baches
man's balls bulging
the beaches, the council-breaching signs
for Ostend Market and
Tahi Road's steely teeth.

She drives the gravel tongue
gorse in her throat
she is learning a new language.
'Song of Myself' plays
along Onetangi highway
two hawks fly the lines
too loud to say in the house but here
the ring is an amphitheatre.

Vineyards applaud
her appearance
green curtains part
and she enters Stage Left.

She wraps her hands
in a pink soliloquy
flicking patois in the mirror
mat trang *jab*
mat wiang san *hook*
sok klap *spinning elbow*
mat wiang klap *spinning backfist*

She is learning a new language.

Her toes pirouette through
black elastic sleeves
her tongue makes way
for the black guard.

She is learning.

A new language gathers in the astropelago of words
strung round her throat
she charts them through her core
belly to shoulder
arms to wrists
during the wai khru ram Muay.

Starry wet tea-towel flicks
through hips, quads, thighs
songs come in rapid bursts
khao trang *straight knee strike*
te tat *roundhouse kick*
thip trang *straight foot thrust*
kradot te *jump kick*

parenthesis to the fury of fists
chok chok chok.

On Saturdays
she learns a new language.

## MASTER TRICKS

Elephant thrusts its tusks
Cross stitch
Bird peeping through nest
Inao stabs Kris

Lifting the summer mountain
Old man holding the melon

Giant steals the girl
Rama pulls arrow string
Break the elephant's tusks
Swan with broken wing

Mon supports the pillar
Impaling the snake
Crocodile sweeps its tail
Break the elephant's neck

Bird somersaults
Deer looks back
Mountain overturns the earth
Extinguish the lamp

Serpent sneaks into the ocean kingdom
Hanuman the monkey king presents the ring

Giant catches the monkey
Tayae supports the pillar
Serpent twists its tail
Java throws a spear

Tiger descends into the stream
Monks sweep the floor
Thread the flower garland
Slice the cucumber

## FLOATING RIBS

*for Panya and Pitisuk K*

The bottom ribs
On both sides
Of the body
Are fragile
Easily broken
They are
Floating ribs
If struck
By a kick with the foot
A knee kick down
From above
A swinging knee kick around
From the side
The result is
Debilitating pain
For the opponent
If the boxer
Delivering the blow
Kicks repeatedly
Floating ribs
Fracture.
And what is this
But life?
Said the Muay Thai master

*Clavicle*
This bone is brittle
Easily broken
Keep this in mind
Always
If it breaks
The shoulder will sag
As happened to Thai boxer
Chatraphetch Kiatkawkeo
Against Kumanthong Lukprabaat
On January 23, 1978.
And what is this
But life?
Said the Muay Thai master

*Solar Plexus*
Even though
This is not
A point to which
A single blow
Can bring a boxer down
Repeated punches
To it
Can be powerfully
Debilitating
Since it lies
Near the heart
It is especially dangerous
If hit hard
Ribs can be broken
Spear the heart
Resulting in death.
And what is this
But life?
Said the Muay Thai master

*Inner Wrist*
This point can be dangerous
In delivering
And receiving blows
In delivering a punch
If not done correctly
It can be
Dislocated
Receiving a kick
May also
Dislocate it.
And what is this
But life?
Said the Muay Thai master

*Shins*
One of the strongest
Parts of the body
Also
Vulnerable
The bone at the centre
On the front
Is brittle
Fractures easily
A powerful blow
As when
You block a kick
Can break it.
And what is this
But life?
Said the Muay Thai master

85

*Point of Chin*
The chin can be reached
With a jumping knee kick
A floating knee kick
Where the left foot
Is raised
From the ground first
Then the right knee thrust up
Powerfully
To the opponent's chin
So that the body leaves the ground
Or with an elbow jab
As Phudphaadnooi Worawuth did
When he won over
Huatrai Sitthi-boonlert
When no one thought
He had the remotest chance
Of winning.
And what is this
But life?
Said the Muay Thai master

*Armpit*
Failure to guard
During a match
Can lead to defeat
A strong upward kick
To it
Can tear the shoulder
Tendons and ligaments
Badly dislocate it.
And what is this
But life?
Said the Muay Thai master

*Philtrum*
The area above
The upper lip
Is a prime spot
For the boxer looking
To knock out his opponent
Close to the nervous system
Like all points close to the nose
When struck it causes tears
To flow
Weakening the opponent.
And what is this
But life?
Said the Muay Thai master

86

*Groin*

In the old days
Eighty years or so ago
Fists were bound with twine
No groin-guards were used
Thai boxers fought without
Shields
Only kapok-stuffed triangular
   cushions
Under loin cloths
The great Thai boxing teacher
Ae Muangdee brought
Metal shields from Singapore
Making it safe from
Hard kicks delivered
With foot or knee
In the opinion of the writer
Anyone not prepared to protect
This part of the body
Should not be a
Thai boxer at all.
And what is this
But life?
Said the Muay Thai master

*Hollow of Knee*

If not protected
If exposed to repeated blows
A boxer can collapse
Lose a match.
And what is this
But life?
And what life
Is this?

This is but life
Said the Muay Thai master

# FIRST SPAR

**I.**
Rosy is sparring

She has won two fights
she has lost two fights

Rosy has two children
her husband has brain cancer

From car to bus to boat
across cool gulf waters
she has come to my island
to be my first spar

Rosy has come very far
Rosy has come to spar

**II.**
Sophie is sparring

Forced in a car
tied to a tree
he leaves
brings one spade
one machete
Sophie, 52 kilos, breaks free
and runs
into 100 kilos of hate
swinging elbow to the eye
jumping knee to the groin
she escapes

He
is still free

She
tries suicide twice

Sophie is sparring for life

III.
Chloe is sparring

A good wife
a good mother
in their twelfth year
he finds another
she leaves a gold ring
and enters a blue one
promising herself
never to disappear again

Chloe has come very far
Chloe has come to spar

IV.
Nita is sparring

She's the CEO
owns the company
her business is equity

She's made of
old-school grit
and when punching the mitt
sees that politician's face
and grins

Nita has come very far
Nita has come to spar

**V.**

Ana is sparring

The funeral is over
mourners have rolled their mats
packed their drum-beaten hearts
folded their flying hands
and left

Ana dances
fatele in the ring
fighting and singing
against bodies
along ropes
in rings

Ana has come very far
Ana has come to spar

# KICKBOXING CANCER

I am the kickboxing woman
I am the Muay Thai woman
I am the woman slipping
I am the woman shadowing
I am the woman jabbing at her own eyes, her own mouth

I am the ringed woman
I am the ringing woman
I am the long-distance-calling woman
I am the short-term memory woman
I am the woman of silence
I am the woman of tossed sheets
Catching the wind of the night
Swallowing the wind of the night

I'm the mourning woman
I'm the teardrop woman
I'm the mourning woman
I'm the fear-dropped woman
I'm the motherless woman
I'm the mothering woman
I'm the sistered woman
The insisting woman
Speaking my mother as I go
Reaching my mother as I go

I am the knowing woman
I am the knotting woman
I am the two hearts woman
I am the scorned woman
I am the woman whose chin refuses to submit
In song, I work in the night
In song, I sing a prayer of terror

I am the cornered woman
I am the woman against the ropes
I am the cornered woman
I rise before the count

I am the still woman
I am the nine-to-five woman
I am the midnight woman
I'm the woman with the pot
I'm the woman with the pen
I'm the woman with the sheaves
A book in every corner as I go
A word in every corner as I go

I am the reading woman
I am the planting woman
I am the fertile woman
The woman with the seeds and water
The woman with the sun and pulling womb
I'm the woman pulling the moon
Pulling Tangaroa as I go
Swimming Tagaloa as I go

I'm the sought-after woman
I'm the seeking woman
I'm the woman skinned with taboos
I'm the censoring woman
I'm the self-censored woman
Rubbing out words as I go
Rubbing out worlds as I go

I'm the poeting woman
I'm the no-poem woman
I'm the coded word woman
I'm the woman with the key

I'm the woman with too many keys
Losing and finding as I go
Trying and opening as I go

I'm the closed-eyed woman
I'm the desired woman
I'm the desiring woman
I'm the shoulder woman
The collarbone woman
I'm the taut pulling and pushing woman

I'm the leaning woman
I am the dreaming woman
I'm the chok woman
I'm the tee sok woman
I'm the teh woman
I'm the tee kao woman
I'm the teep woman
Punching and kicking as I go
Grappling and clinching as I go

I'm the take-out woman
I'm the fake-out woman
I'm the art-of-eight-limbs woman
I'm the spinning backfist woman
I'm the elbow thrust, driving knee, roundhouse kick woman

I'm the ab-flexed woman
I'm the resting next woman
I'm the next best woman
I'm the winning woman

I'm the stalking woman
I'm the keep-walking-forward woman
I'm the push kick woman
I'm the jab jab hook woman

Wiping my sweat as I go
Wiping blood as I go

I'm the pressed-earth woman
I'm the pressed-lipped woman
I'm the held and kept woman
I'm the leapt woman
I'm gone and going as I go
I stay behind as I go

I'm the woman with her weight on her back foot
I'm the woman with her weight on her front foot
I'm the woman springing
I'm singing her blues
I'm the core muscle woman
I'm the torn muscle woman
I'm the woman with the pages
I'm the woman in the pages
I'm the woman in the man
His pupil, my sight

I'm the woman with the tattoos
I'm the woman with the pierced belly
I'm the woman with the tattoos
I'm the woman piercing tongues
Culling words as I go
Culling worlds as I go

I'm the woman with the script
I'm the woman in the lead
I'm the woman storming out
I'm the woman storming in
I'm the kickboxing woman
I'm the Muay Thai woman

Sparring myself as I go
Shadowing myself as I go

# ANNIVERSARY

What if grief were a Sky Tower bungy jump?
Having wrapped you up in gear for a year
death's anniversary comes round with a Use It or Lose It ticket
and you've got this one tippy-toeing shot to shoot into the Va
between you and the Gone-Her
and cabled by the restraints of the flesh
could you fly with God for eight secs flat?

What if mourning were a tandem jumper with a virgin
leaper? Keeper of fateful-day memories secured in your
pack and the only way to unlatch it all was to
hatch it all through the open mouth of a plane from 12,000 feet where
the Lego world waited beneath, incomplete?

What if depression were a Muay Thai tournament? And the lineament
    had gotten in
your eyes, and the pit was disguised as a red and blue ring and you only
    realised
once inside, strapped, gloved and ready to rumble with the undefeated
of All Time, that you couldn't breathe, that it was a year too early
and you needed to leave because you were a novice and really didn't
    know anything?

What if the last day of the first month of the first year came
and went
and you did nothing you'd said you'd do
and grief, mourning, depression
twelve months of tightly coiled elastic bands had slackened
had become a little less swift with its spring-back sting?

## SALT

As if God spilt salt
on his midnight tablecloth
as if Gibran's Ugly
had flung Beauty's cloak
across the waters –
its soft light muted
in repentance
as if star by blue star
remembered the loss of each mother
and lit her face for a thousand years
as if Matariki
leapt off calendar pages
turning in my veins
down through my fingers
bending to pluck
a purple orchid.

*Acknowledgements*

Fa'afetai tele lava to the editors of the following books, magazines, websites, exhibitions and events where some of these poems previously appeared: *The World Record: International Voices from Southbank Centre's Poetry Parnassus* (Bloodaxe Books); *Pacific Identities and Well-Being: Cross-Cultural Perspectives* (Routledge); Rain of Poems, London (Casagrande); *Landfall* (Otago University Press); *SPAN: Journal of the South Pacific Association for Commonwealth Literature and Language Studies*; *Cordite Poetry Review*; *Shenandoah: The Washington and Lee University Review*; the New Zealand Electronic Poetry Centre (nzepc); *Leaders Magazine* (Leadership New Zealand Pumanawa Kaiarahi O Aotearoa); Wild Lines Dunedin, Dunedin Fringe Festival; and the International Women's Day Maori Art Space exhibition at Waikare Art Gallery.

Fa'afetai tele lava to Anna Hodge, a most thoughtful editor; to Katrina Duncan and the brilliant team at Auckland University Press; to musician Tim Page, whose original and responsive rhythms widen the audience for poetry; to Moe Alefaio for help with Tuvaluan translations; and to the remarkable Lonnie Hutchinson for sharing her artwork *Before Sunrise* (2010) on the cover. While symbolically nodding to Matariki, *Before Sunrise* also bears a striking resemblance to my inner Pasifika-fairy shadow sparring self.

Fa'afetai tele lava to Jules and that first text message introducing me to Duan and the world of Marshall Arts Kickboxing, Waiheke Island; to my fellow kick-butt partners over the years – Aleysha, Emma, Donna, Erin, Joyce, Anna, Kylie, Michelle, Denis, Cheryl, Karen, Camilla, Trina, Ruby and Anita; to my life sparring partner, David; and to Javan, Annalina, Micah, Davey, Luka and Cinzia, who must now contend in a world without their fighting Nana Crosbie.

*Track list*

| | | |
|---|---|---|
| 1. | Matariki | 3.13 |
| 2. | Chant from Matiatia to Orapiu | 4.49 |
| 3. | Emailing Albert | 2.32 |
| 4. | Lead | 4.38 |
| 5. | New Zealand, the lucky country | 10.38 |
| 6. | On plagiarism | 3.05 |
| 7. | Noose | 2.22 |
| 8. | Boxing | 2.08 |
| 9. | Fatele | 3.26 |
| 10. | Muay Thai on Saturdays | 2.59 |
| 11. | First spar | 3.23 |
| 12. | Kickboxing cancer | 5.41 |
| 13. | Salt | 1.06 |